Bell Michael

Joseph Antonaccio Oral History Interview

Bell Michael

Joseph Antonaccio Oral History Interview

ISBN/EAN: 9783337300784

Printed in Europe, USA, Canada, Australia, Japan

Cover: Foto ©Andreas Hilbeck / pixelio.de

More available books at **www.hansebooks.com**

UNIVERSITY OF MASSACHUSETTS LOWELL
CENTER FOR LOWELL HISTORY
ORAL HISTORY COLLECTION

LIBRARY OF CONGRESS
AMERICAN FOLKLIFE CENTER
ORAL HISTORY PROJECT

NFORMANT: JOE ANTONACCIO
CONDUCTED BY: MICHAEL BELL
DATE: NOVEMBER 16, 1987

B = MICHAEL BELL
A = JOE ANTONACCIO

LFP MB-R010-R011

B: To make sure it's working. Let's see, today is November the 16th, 1987. My name's Michael Bell, and I'm interviewing for the Lowell Folklife Project.

A: Joe Antonaccio.

B: Okay, that sounds good. Well why don't we start with the question that you asked me. Like where, where you grew up? Where you came from?

A: Oh, okay. I was ah, born, raised in Mt. Vernon, New York. And um, I guess about the age of nine my ah, parents moved us down into New York City, about one block away from Chinatown and stayed there until I was twelve, then moved back to Mt. Vernon. I think that three year period in, near Chinatown had a lasting impact on my life. When I was nineteen years old, joined the Air Force. After I joined the Air Force I got married to an American woman, had two kids by her. Then I got shipped over to Thailand. And ah, I was there for a year. Got out of the service. I guess ah, got divorced a year later. And got remarried a year later after that to the same woman. [laugh]

B: I'm not going to say it. [laugh]

A: Yeah, and lived together about ten years more, then we finally separate and went our separate ways. I came up to ah, Stone, Stoneham, Massachusetts. Director of Corporate Communications for a High-Tech Company in ah, Wakefield. And I guess I was single for about five years. Then I met my present wife who's a Laotian Refugee. I ah, graduated from New York University with a Bachelors Electrical Electronics Engineering. I have a couple of patents. One with N.C.R. One with [Wheelocks?] Signals in Long Branch, New Jersey. Had ah, very promising career in electronics. And ah, after I got married to my Laotian wife um, I had started my ah, Engineering Consulting Company I guess in 1979, or 80. I don't remember which. I think 1980. And ah, met my Laotian wife and we started going from here to Hartford, Connecticut to visit her folks, or her relatives, but not her folks. Her relatives lived in ah, Hartford. And every weekend that we went down there they would ask us to stop in Boston Chinatown and pick-up groceries for them. Now, I had grown up in New York City so I knew where the wholesalers were. And one weekend I said to her, "why don't we go down to New York City and ah, load up a van full of this stuff and bring it into Hartford and sell it to all the refugees that are beginning to come and settle into Hartford area." And that was the beginning of our business. Ah, we opened up our first retail grocery store in December, I think, of '81. We opened another one in ah, I think '83, in Hartford. Then in '84 we opened another one [phone rings in back ground] in ah, hold on [tape is shut off] We opened a third one a year later in Winsocket, R.I. And um, the same, let's see, a year later we opened the a restaurant, and that same year we closed the Winsocket Retail Store.

B: I was going to ask you. Is there much of an Asian Community in Winsocket?

A: Winsocket.

B: Providence is, I live in Providence.

A: Uh, they have quite, quite a population in Providence. I think a lot of those people have come up this way too, (B: Yeah) because there's lots more jobs up here. There was at that time maybe four thousand, maybe, no not that many. Maybe, maybe two thousand in um, Winsocket. And ah, it just wasn't enough to support an operation the size that we like to run them. So we gave that up and we opened up the restaurant. December 15th of this year we're closing on the purchase of a manufacturing facility. And we're going to be manufacturing Asian food products meat products all U.S.A. approved stuff. And we'll be selling it into the Asian Community, as well as into the American Market.

B: What food?

A: Chinese sausage, Laotian sausage, Cambodian sausage. Ah, Giozas, that's the wonton.

B: Oh, okayed. Meat filled?

A: Meat filled products, right. Steamed buns, Spring Rolls, ah, Sweet Meat, Jerky, have about twelve, thirteen different items that we plan to manufacture, in addition to the American product that the company that we're buying is presently manufacturing. So we're going into an operation that's already successful, and we just compared more products to it. And that will take place some time in December. Um, want to know a little bit about the Asian food? Um, I lived in Thailand for a year when I was in the Air Force. And um, unfortunately I didn't get a chance to travel into Burma or Cambodia, or ah, or Laos. It wasn't until I came back to the states and ah, got very actively involved with the refugees, did I realize that while they may have separate languages there's a root within the language that can be traced back to ah, Sanskrit and ah, Bali and ah, of course the religion came from India. Over through what is present day what, Bangladesh? The old Pakistan I guess, right? And um, in through Burma. Spread down south in Burma. There were two passes one in the north, one in the south. Where it got into Thailand. Spread in the northern part of Thailand, the southern part of Thailand, and it went all the way down in through Malaysia. That was the original, I guess that was the um, original Buddhism or Hinduism, okay, and spread into Cambodia. I guess it spread into Cambodia at the time of Angkor when they had the

B: Angkor Wat?

J: Angkor Wat, when Cambodia was at its peak. And it spread into Vietnam. But I think in Vietnam it didn't, it didn't um, grab hold, as well as it did in the other countries. And also had another interest coming into Vietnam. They had China from the northern part. So ah, there is a commonalty in language. Between Thai and Laotian there's probably a 30% overlap in the language. If you understand, if you're an educated person in Laos for example, you can understand almost all of the Thai.

B: But not Cam, not the Khmer.

J: You can understand if you're educated and you're, and you're interested in understanding you can probably pick up 20% of it.

B: Really?

J: If you're not educated, and racists, and prejudice like ah, and of course it's just a brup, brup, brup, and no, no sounds, you know.

B: Yeah, that's why I interviewed all Laotian.

J: Ah ha.

B: Here. And he said ah, Cambodian and Laotian are totally different languages. [Unclear]

J: They are totally different, but there is a root. There is that root that, that ah, there are some old words in the Cambodian, ah, in the Laotian language. If you know those old words, you can pick up Cambodian.

B: So it might be like ah, French is to English or even closer? (J: Ah, yeah) I mean they're cognates.

J: Sure.

B: You can understand.

J: Matter of fact, when my wife says a word to me in Laotian and I don't understand it, she'll say it to me in Thai. If I don't understand it in Thai, she'll go to French. And invariably I can always get it when it's said to me in French, because it's very close communique for communications, you know?

B: Now how's your wife's English?

J: My wife's English is reasonable, reasonable. I mean she's not ah, she doesn't practice it at all, because I speak Laos at the house all the time. And um, my son who's 5 1/2 (--)

B: His name is Douglas?

J: Yeah, he speaks Laos and he speaks Thai.

B: And English?

J: English he speaks well, because he's, actually before he went to day care he didn't speak a word of English.

B: Oh!

J: And that was at age four we sent him to day care and ah, now he prefers English over the rest because of the (--)

B: Everybody else.

J: all the peer pressure I guess. We have Cambodians that work in the store with us, as well as Laotians. And um, we all tend to share the language. You know we all pick up a little bit of each others language. And um, it is surprising, because there are a lot of words that we can understand. You know out of the Cambodian, if they listen closely they can pick up words out of the ah, the Thai or the Laos. It depends upon what we're, what we're speaking to them. The food, I know that's where you want to go, into the food.

B: Well, yeah, but it all fits. I mean.

J: Oh yeah, yeah.

B: You can't isolate a food from culture.

J: That's right. The ah, the food, the basic ingredients throughout all of South East Asia, are the same in all the countries. Okay. ah, hot chili peppers, predominant in Vietnam, Laos, Cambodia and Thai and Burma.

B: And Louisiana too. [laughter]

J: And even Louisiana, yeah.

B: Hot chili.

J: So hot chili peppers, ah lemon grass, ah curries, um [coughs].

B: Are their chilies different? I mean there are so many, there are different varieties of chilies. Like is there a special kind?

J: Yeah, I don't know, there's a, there's a Latin name for their chili, but they call them Pikineau. Pikineau means um, pepper, little mouse. Little mouse pepper, Pikineau. And, but if they, if they, if they use a translation ah, they don't, they may say Pikineau, but doesn't, the direct translation is "little mouse pepper." But when they, when they translate it into English they'll say, "bird pepper", because it doesn't sound very nice to say mouse pepper. [coughs] Ah, but they're blistering hot. I don't think there's any pepper ah (--)

B: Do you get them whole?

J: Yeah. We get them out of Florida.

B: How big are they? Are they like (--)

J: They're about as big as your pinky.

B: Okay. They're (--)

J: Sometimes smaller. [coughs] We um, (B: and they're) they're the hottest pepper known to man. I'm sure of it.

B: And they're red when they're picked?

J: Red and green, lot's of (--)

B: The red ones are just riper, right?

J: Right. And the hottest time of the year for the chili peppers is about August and September when they're ripening on the vine. September they clear out the, all the peppers off the bushes. And most of them are red at that time. And ah, we won't see fresh peppers out of Florida until say ah, March again.

B: So that's when most of them are grown?

J: Most of them are being grown in Florida, North Carolina, New Jersey.

B: Just for the, just for the South East Asian Community basically?

J: Yeah, umhm. A lot of Thai Nationals married American G.I's, and um, came to America with them at, in the '75's. And I guess throughout the 60's and right up to the 80's. And um, they're, they started little gardens and before you know it the refugees started coming in in '75. And these, lots of Thai women that I know of are growing these things in their own back yards and selling them to the local markets. They will grow as north as Massachusetts. You can probably find a little bit of it into New Hampshire. They need a long growing season. One hundred and twenty days, you don't get that up here too often. Um, Thai eggplants. Lots of exotic vegetables that you don't find ah,

B: Now, what's the, what's the difference between a Thai eggplant and say a regular old, the kind you would see in eggplant parmesan, or something.

J: Doesn't, doesn't even look, doesn't even look like an eggplant.

B: No. It's not darker?

J: It's a little round green ball, smaller than a golf ball. Sometimes about the same size as a golf ball. And the only way that you would even look at it and say that it could possibly be an eggplant, is if you cut it open and there's trillions of seeds in it. That's the only way, okay.

B: But taste?

J: Taste wise nothing. It's, it's almost neutral. It will absorb the flavors of whatever you're, (B: okay) you're cooking with it. Um, I did have a ah, a nice article that I wrote ah, for the restaurant. I talked a little bit about the potpourri of flavors that you have. Ah, in throughout South East Asia. Um, the curries came in with Buddhism. I'm sure of that.

B: From India.

J: From India. Um

B: The curry itself is just a combination of like ah (--)

J: It's cloves.

B: Pepper, or ah, [unclear] pepper, whatever.

J: Yeah. Cloves, turmeric ah, or turmeric, um, Thyme, a couple of different spices mixed together. And um, but it came in through that, through that, with that, with that wave I'm quite sure. And um, the Thai people and the Burmese people are very clever with curries. Tend to, it tends to have stopped over there. It didn't really go into ah, Cambodia and Laos and ah, get absorbed into their national dishes. It stopped in Thailand for some reason. I don't know why. Ah, every country has what they consider to be their national dish. Ah, for example in Laos the national dish is Laop. And Laop is fresh beef, chopped with a knife, very fine, mixed with mint, um, pork stomach, beef stomach, ah chili peppers, lemon, a thing called bladak, which is pickled fish. And very, very tasty.

B: Some kind of stew?

J: Ah, it's just, it could be raw, or it could just, water passed through it very quickly.

B: Ha.

J: So it's almost eaten raw. This is called Laop. This is the national dish of Laos, Laop. The, probably the national dish in Thailand ah, well, there's a couple of them. But ah, I would think probably, Tom-Yum-Gong. Tom-Yum. Tom-Yum is a soup, Gong is shrimp. It's a hot and sour shrimp soup. Um, in Cambodia they also have a hot and sour ah, fish soup and they call it ah, Som-Lau-Mijutri. If, between those three countries they each know each other's national dishes. And they have a different name for it. And that was the jest of the, the frontest piece of my menu. (B: Oh, okay) Okay. That ah, even though they have their own identities their cooking styles are very similar to one another. Ah, they have a wide range of, of ah, vegetables. Ah, from which to, to draw upon. They have lot's of different spices that they use. And they all use pretty much the same spices in their cooking, but in varying degrees. The Laotians love it blistering hot. As do the Thais. The Cambodian's like it a little bit milder, whatever it is that they're cooking, okay. On the other hand the Cambodians like the real strong fish flavor. Whereas the ah, the fish flavor and the sour. Whereas in the, in the, Laotian's may like the heavy fish flavor, but they would want it ah, not sour but ah, hot, okay. Fish and hot. So just to give you an example the, there's a very popular dish that all three of them eat and it's, it's a wide rice noodles, quick fried with an egg, put on a plate. And then a topping of ah, broccoli, baby corn, mushrooms, and some meat, and stewed in it's own gravy, and put on top of those rice noodles. In Thai they call that, Guitio Lat Na. In Laos they call it For Kor. And in Cambodian they call it ah, Miktong, but it's the identical dish in all three countries.

B: Just slightly different spices?

J: Not even slightly different. It's exactly the same.

B: Hm.

J: As I said they all know each others National Dish. That happens to be a Chinese dish. And they've just (--)

B: Yeah, it's got (--)

J: They've all taken that Chinese dish and they've you know

B: I've had that. A similar thing in Chinese Restaurants.

J: Now, there's another one (--)

B: Especially with the baby corn and the broc, and the broccoli and the mushrooms. (J: Yeah) Sometimes it's on noodles.

J: This is a wide rice noodle that it's on.

B: Yeah, or I mean the skinny (--)

J: Thin noodles, yeah. (B: Yeah, [unclear]) We could do that on, on a thin yellow noodle. Then it would be called Brami, Brami Lung Lat Na, in the Thai language. Um, the, a very popular dish through out all of China all of Taiwan, Korea, um Malaysia, Thailand, Laos, Cambodia, Vietnam, Burma, is a thing called ah, the Vietnamese call it Fah. And it's a soup. Okay, that's, this is the the Nation, that's the soup that everyone eats. They eat it for breakfast, lunch, or supper. Very popular in the morning. It's a noodle soup. Rice noodles, if it, if it's in South East Asia that you're eating this, when you eat, eat it with rice noodles. If it's in Korea or um, China, they like it with ah, wheat noodles. If you eat it in Taiwan they'll have a different, they'll have a flat wheat noodle. But it's the identical soup. Ah, it's a beef broth soup. Ah, bean sprouts in it, thin rice noodles, or wheat noodles, ah, some fried garlic that we fry up ahead of time and have it sitting aside and just put it into the soup. Um, would have scallions, coriander. The meat of your choice, or um, shrimp and squid. Okay. And it's a meal. All by itself it's a meal. The Vietnamese call it Fah, the Laotians call it Fah, they stole the Vietnamese word. The Thai people call it Quitio Nam. Nam means water, and Quitio means noodle. So Quitio Nam. And the Cambodians all it Quitio Tuk. The Quitio again means noodle. Same word as in Thai and in Laos. And Tuk means water. So, there's the soup. And everybody knows the soup no matter what country comes, you know, where they come from they know that soup. There are a number of dishes that everyone knows. And those are the dishes that we have on our menu. And um (--)

B: In, in variations.

J: Yeah. We, we also have some you know, strictly ah, Thai dishes, some strictly Laos dishes, and ah Vietnamese dishes, but generally we try to keep the dishes that all of the nationalities know. My whole concept in the restaurant was to open it up for the Asian people. We came to Lowell, there were no retail grocery stores. We were the first one to open.

B: That was what, 1981?
J: In 81, right. December of 81. And they came into our store. They helped us to grow. We, we serviced them very well. They, they, and ah, in return for that I feel as though we owe them something. Okay. So we opened up the restaurant. We opened up the restaurant, and the prices in the restaurant are lower than you find anywhere else. The food is very authentic. The ambiance is strictly Asian. [laugh] You know, I put some wallpaper on one wall just to keep the Americans happy. And, and our attitude right in the very beginning was, this is for the Asians. And if the Americans happen to find it, all well and good. If they don't find it, I'm not going to go out of my way for them. Because the whole, the whole concept was strictly an Asian Restaurant. And it's worked very well. Of course we don't get the ah, ah, Americans you know, with their evening gowns and suits on, (B: right) but who needs them anyway.

B: Yeah, I was going to say, if that happens do you think it would ah, change the character? Would the Asians stop coming?

J: The Asians would stop coming.

B: Would they?

J: Yeah, even though the food is right. They would not come. Because ah,

B: A lot of Americans came without evening dress.

J: Well, they, they, they, the Americ, the Asians know that the lunch hour is just jammed with Americans. And they don't even bother coming at lunch hour. They'll come right up until lunch hour. And they'll come right after lunch hour. But they won't come in while the Americans are in there at lunch hour for some reason, I don't know why. I guess, you know, they have their, their time slots. And um, the concepts work very well in so far as I'm concerned and ah, I wouldn't change anything in the restaurant. If I did put a, another restaurant up I might gear it more towards the Americans, because the Asians have their restaurant now. So if I did another one it would be for the Americans. And I wouldn't change the food of course. But um (--)

B: What kind of research did you have to do to get, I mean did you just talk to people in the community? Or did you, uh, you know, read about different foods and so on? [Unclear]

J: When we opened the restaurant you mean?

B: Yeah, in terms of researching like [unclear] to the people, or (--) I know you were, you were already selling groceries.

J: When I went to Thailand, I had lived there in Thailand for a year you have to remember.

B: Right.

J: And ah, ah, I used to go down to the market place ah, every day as a matter of fact. And I would watch the venders cooking these foods. And I had my favorite dishes. And I wrote down every single recipe that I ever saw over there. Okay. So when it was time to do the restaurant I had, you know, I remembered this.

B: And you were making the food for yourself anyway.

J: Yeah. Through the ensuing twenty years after I got back from Thailand. And ah, when it came time to open the restaurant, of course I had the dishes that I liked. And I said to my wife, "well here's what we'll put on the menu, we'll put this, this, this, this and this." And my wife said, "Oh, you have to have this, this, this and this." So before you knew it we had probably fifteen items on the menu. Then we hired ah, an old woman ah, Laotian woman and she says, "well you don't have this on it." So we were to put this, this, this and this on it.

B: So you had to make that, right?

J: Yeah, and then we hired another woman that had some experience working in a restaurant in Bangkok. And she said, "Oh, you're missing this, this, this and this." Before you knew it we had one hundred and five things on the menu.

B: Yeah it's a big menu. [Chuckles]

J: Yeah.

J: And ah, all good stuff. Every bit of it's good. There, there are a couple of things that we're going to take off on the second ah, pass. Things that are just really too strong for the ah, American palate. They're too strong for the Laotian palate, they're too strong for the Thai palate. Only the Cambodians will eat it.

B: Is it very fishy?

J: Yeah. But they will ask for it if they want it.

B: Oh.

J: They never read our menus anyway. They just ask us directly.

B: That's interesting.

J: Yeah. Even though it's written. We have the menus written in Cambodian. They'll, they never even read them, they just say, "oh, can you make us this?" Sure we can make it.

B: So what will you do, like a special dish for someone who comes in?

J: Anything, sure.

B: And describes it. If you've never heard of it, they'd say well, it's this, this, this and that.

J: We'll try it.

B: You'll try it?

J: Yeah, we try anything.

B: That's interesting.

J: We're not afraid to try it. The Asians in particular appreciate that too. I'm what, I some what of an oddity over here in the community, because I speak ah, Thai, and I speak Laos, speak a little bit of Cambodian, and ah, I know that I cook better than probably half the people in the community. Ah, they see me cooking and they know that I cook very well. And they come in and they always, some of them want me to cook for them. They don't want the Laotians to cook for them, or someone else. You know, they specifically want me to cook for them. So I'm somewhat of an oddity. And ah, you know it's fun.

B: How often are you ah, cooking?

J: Ah, on lunch hours I usually go in and help. Ah, Saturdays or Sundays. I'm always there on

Sunday, at least a half a day. When we first opened up the restaurant I was there all the time. And ah, now I've, we've expanded the business. I still do a little bit of engineering on the side. Still do some computer programming. Matter of fact I just had a call just before you came in. I've got two more programs that I have to write. Very little time in the day. [Chuckles]

B: It must be things you like to do though, or you wouldn't (--)

J: Yeah. You know, you know.

B: You wouldn't do it.

J: I remember hearing a, one time someone said, "if you want something done give it to a busy guy." He'll find a way to get it done, because that's just his nature. That's me, that's my nature. I get up at five-thirty in the morning, five o'clock, sometimes four o'clock I'm here. And ah, I go to bed eleven-thirty, twelve o'clock. I don't need much sleep. And ah, play with the computer. Do the programming in the early morning hours. Up until about seven then start to, doing my bookkeeping until about nine, and run

B: And that's all computerized, right?

J: Yeah, everything is computerized.

B: How about in the store? In the restaurant?

J: That's all computerized too. The ah, inventories all computerized, all my ordering.

B: You have all your ah, menus and everything all (--)

J: That's on the word processing.

B: Yeah, word processing.

J: Yeah, yeah. And ah, I guess from nine o'clock, after we hit the bank and come back, from then on we're just sort of snooping around seeing what's going on. You know, help this one, help that one. Make sure things are getting done the way I want it done.

B: By nine o'clock in the morning?

J: Nine o'clock in the morning, yeah. We open ah, the doors for business in the restaurant at nine, between nine and nine-thirty. The doors at the retail store open at nine-thirty on the button. We close the retail store down at eight. Close the restaurant down at nine-thirty, and we're there until ten, quarter after ten, and go home. We never cook at home any more. We always eat in the restaurant. Or occasionally like today, we went out and ate pizza. [laugh]

B: Oh, you know, I was going to ask you about, because ah, talking to South East Asians in Lowell, they mix. Like everything, food is ah, you know, they'll eat Kentucky Fried Chicken (J:

Oh, yeah) and then maybe have traditional food at home, or something, or somewhere else.

J: I think if, if you looked at the priorities of ah, the community you would find out that their most important priority of course is going to be food. Second most important priority is going to be a car, good automobile. Third important, or third in their list of priorities would probably be clothing, and the last would be where they live. And ah, I think most Americans don't understand this. Most Americans say jeese, they're getting real big handout being on welfare, look at this they've all got brand new cars, you know. The Americans don't realize that the reason that they're able to do this is because they have their priorities set different than Americans. They're, they're content to live two or three families in a single apartment. So that where an apartment might cost the single American four hundred and fifty dollars a month, these people would divide that by three. (B: Yeah) Okay. And another very important feature of their community is that when a member of the family wants to buy an automobile, you got to remember that it benefits the entire group that's living in the same building. So they can go out and borrow money from everybody.

B: They on, they probably only need one.

J: They only need one car.

B: One per house hold? Right? [Unclear]

J: Yeah, and after they get that one car it gives them the mobility to work two and three jobs. And they've got the reliable transportation, cause there's usually a brand new car. And they're all helping to pay it off.

B: The Trans-am. [Comment unclear]

J: Sure. They've got a lot of nice cars. The younger, the young kids have a lot.

B: Yeah, I've noticed, I've noticed that.

J: But ah, even the, the um, you know the family, family oriented ah, members of the community will buy new cars, and you're not going to be dumping a lot of money into them to repair them and fix them all the time. They recognize right off the bat you know, that you need that in this country. In their own country they were on foot power. Over here they have the mobility to go get jobs anywhere they want them. They're not adversed to working two shifts, back to back. It's not uncommon to see a husband working two shifts, and his wife working two shifts with one of them over lapping while the kids are in school. And between, if, if ah, if it's a family that maybe the kids are seventeen, eighteen, nineteen or twenty years old, you've got three incomes out of six jobs.

B: Right.

J: You know? They're beginning to buy property, you know, and they're moving. They're moving in the community. They're moving up the economic ladder. I think that ah, lot's of

American's are jealous over this. But they don't understand why. How, how's it happening? They think it's all welfare. They're so, you know, so wrong.

B: But they won't talk to them to find out.

I: Yeah. Yeah, they won't talk to them.

B: So, do you think they're is a barrier between ah, the Asian Community and ah, the non-Asian Community?

I: I, I think there is a great deal of prejudice in the city of Lowell. As an American, I mean I don't always have my wife by my side.

B: Umhm.

I: All right. Um, so I think that I, I feel it more than the average person would. Since she's not always by my side, if I'm out doing something and people don't know who I am, inevitably I'll hear something, you know, "damn Gooks, or slant eyes," or what have you. You know, they don't even know that they're Cambodian, or Vietnamese, or Laos. They just call them you know, all the Chinks. (B: Right) And um, I find that with the older Greek people, is where you have a great deal of ah, prejudice. This is going to be public, but that's okay.

B: Yeah. No, it's the truth from your perspective anyways.

I: It's the truth! [Chuckles] When I first moved into this building I had an old woman come up to the door. She was a little tipsy at the time. And she said, "oh, you bought the old Greek market? You're going to keep it all Greek again?" I says, "no, I'm not going to keep it Greek anymore." She said, "oh, what are you going to do?" I said, "I'm going to do Chinese food." You wouldn't believe the vulgarities that came out of this woman's mouth. She told me she was going to blow the place up. Her husband had served in Vietnam, as a Marine, and he was, they hang out at the Cosmo, and they were going to blow me away. That all went away very quickly though. But ah, we do wedding receptions for the Asians, ah, in the parking lot over there. And ah, there's about, at least on three separate occasions, little old Greek woman have come by, "oh, what are you doing." You know, and we tell them what we're doing. And ah, "oh, someone's getting married. Who's getting married?" "Uh, some Cambodian." "Cambodians! Ha, they ought to go back where they came from." You know.

B: It's like a short memory.

I: Yeah, it is. They had, they were refugees at one time and they had to fight off the, the French Canadians and the Irish, you know. But that's the one group that I feel is still the most prejudice of all.

B: The Cambodians are pretty much going through, or the Asians are going through what other ethnic groups had to go through.

J: Except that the, the ah, Asian community over here (--)

Side I ends
Side II begins

J: The real difference between the, the Asians and the other ethnic groups, ah (--) Of course the other ethnic groups came here. They didn't, they had to work, in order to get their first piece of bread on the table. They didn't have welfare, they didn't have all of the programs that the federal government have set up now, okay. So understandably they're a bit jealous, the, the other, the other groups.

B: Right.

J: They're jealous because the Asians have it a little easier, in so far as um, getting their, their foothold. Ah, but even if the Asians didn't have that slight bit of advantage, I think that the Asians would still over come and, and far outpace the other ethnic groups, because of the environment they came from. Okay. You had to go out and hustle in order to survive in the Asian countries, okay. Um, they're, it's an Agrarian Society. So that means every day you're out there looking for food. Okay, everyday you're out there in the field, either growing your own foods or foraging for foods. Um, if you forage for ah, and have a surplus of foods, you take that into town and you barter and you get your meats, or you barter and you get your ah, clothing, or cloth. Ah, if you happen to have a, a, be fortunate enough and raise a few pigs, you'll take one o those into town and barter and get whatever else you need. Okay. So, independent I think of um, the notion that they are receiving welfare, I think that they would have moved up our economic scale much quicker than any other group preceding them in spite of what was you know, ah, in spite of what the pressures might have been.

B: I guess you can put them next to other, not even as recent groups who haven't done as well.

J: Umhm.

B: And see the difference.

J: Yeah. Yeah. Within five years there are more, I think there are probably more percentage of Asians owning houses than any other group prior to them. I'm pretty sure of that. A lot of homes are being bought by the Asians. Now of course the price of housing is just so incredibly high that they can't even come up with the down payments anymore. Not even Americans can come up with down payments, but ah, prior to ah, this last round of buy, of a sellers market ah, they had bought up a lot of the you know, older buildings and ah, they're making some (--)

B: Multi-family

J: Yeah, multi-family units and they're making money on them.

B: Now where have they mainly settled? In the [unclear]

J: Yeah, in the uh, in and around the Acre area. Um, Thorndike Street is a very heavy population, or a heavy density of them. Um, the Acre, which is Broadway. On the other side of town along Mill Street, Newhall Street.

B: Okay. I have a vague understanding of some of the neighborhoods.

J: Wherever there was low income housing that's where they settled.

B: Okay. The Acre is basically what, in through here?

J: The Acre is bounded by um, Adams Street, Broadway, Thorndike, um, I don't know the name of the street that runs along the canal.

B: Ah, wait a minute, I'll see. You mean the southern edge?

J: Ah, where we at right now?

B: Which canal? Okay, well there's City Hall. So were (--)

J: Okay, City Hall.

B: We might, is this the Acre right in here?

J: Yes. All in this area right in here. This whole area. And here's Fletcher Street, Adams Street. (B: Umhm) Now where's Broadway? Here's Market Street. That's the street right out in front of me. (B: Right) So it goes all the way up to the end and it turns into Salem. Runs down Fletcher. It's a triangle.

B: Oh, okay. So this is, this is a pretty small area.

J: Yeah, well that's, there's a high concentration of ah, of the Asian refugees, as well as Hispanics in that area. And mostly because it's very low income housing.

B: Okay. Some projects, or some public housing there?

J: Yeah, public housing. Ah, there's a lot of drugs in that area, which the Asians are not participating in. At least not to my knowledge. Um, then you have some other public housing down on, in the French Street area. Um, let's see, all along, up and down in here. Moody Street, in back there's public housing. There's a lot of Vietnamese have settle into that area. There's probably about 120 families, no not even that many. That's way off. Ah, 150 Vietnamese people in the City of Lowell. Maybe 200.

B: So it's probably the smallest of the (--)

J: It is.

B: the four.

J: There is about 8 or 9,000 Cambodians, 3 or 4,000 Laotians.

B: And Thai?

J: Very few Thai. Any Thais that are in the area probably live out of Lowell. Married to American G.I's, or American servicemen.

B: It's not like a community.

J: No. No. They're all over. There is a, a sizable population of Thai people up in the ah, some down in the Fort Deven's area, And some up near the air force base up in ah, I think Pease Air Force Base. Up in ah, what is that? In Maine? And they come down here to do all their shopping since we're the first store around. (B: Oh, that's interesting) There are eight other stores besides myself, or seven other stores.

B: In Lowell?

J: In Lowell now. We were the first to open in 81. Um, the second one opened up in 83, and every year thereafter they just sprouted like flower.

B: They're just like Asian, they're just Asian markets?

J: All Asian markets, yeah. Run by Chinese Cambodians.

B: Chinese Cambodians?

J: Yup.

B: And they keep separate from, are they distinct?

J: They like to believe that they're part of the community, but the real Cambodian doesn't accept them that well. [laughs] If he's Chinese Cambodian he says well, he's Chinese. You know.

B: Were they like immigrants?

J: The ah, yeah they came here as refugees also.

B: From Cambodia?

J: From Cambodia. They were probably born into Chinese, you know, the Chinese families um they're what they call overseas Chinese. These are Chinese people that have migrated out of mainland China, moved into Cambodia, Laos, Thailand

B: So it's, that was relatively recent though, after the revolution in, after '49.

J: Right, and so ah, two or three generations have passed, actually two or three generations have started since then. Okay. every what, every 10 years? Or every, every, yeah, I guess every 10 years you might start a new generation. I don't know what the regulation is for (--)

B: I used (--) We used to think of it as 30, but I don't, that just doesn't seem (--)

J: [Chuckles] That's too big. (B: Too long, yeah) That's too wide a gap, yeah. Because certainly, I think generation is, has a lot to do with how you perceive your elders.

B: That's it, things have changed, are changing so rapidly, that a generation, I mean there's a gap now.

J: Yeah.

B: In sort of ten years.

J: Anyways these, some of the old time Chinese people moved into Laos, and Cambodia, and Thailand, and Vietnam and they raised their families and those people raised their families, okay. And what you have over here then is ah, Chinese people who are probably held Cambodian citizenship. If you can consider that they would have citizenship the same way we do. If you're born in this country you're automatically an American citizen. But I know it's not true. In Cambodia if you're born over there it doesn't mean that you're a citizen of Cambodia. You have to be Cambodian if you're going to be a citizen. Ah, you can be a Chinese ah, Cambodian meaning that you are of Chinese blood, but born in Cambodia. Um, they're, the Chinese are very akin to the, to the American Jew, or the Jews in Europe. They revor education. They're, they're usually the merchants, (B: right) ownership. They don't particularly care about land, but they do care about the movement of goods. Okay. What would you call it, the mercantile?

B: Yeah, the traders.

J: Traders. And um, they're very good with it. They're very good with it. They can establish the pipelines for ah, getting their supplies. And if they speak one dialect, or two dialects of Chinese no matter where they go in the world they can communicate.

B: Are there a significant number of Chinese Cambodians?

J: Yeah, I'd say that probably 5% of the population is Chinese Cambodian. And ah, Laotian Chinese, we have those too. They're born in Laos, but they're really Chinese. And they'll call themselves you know, Laotian. They speak two or three languages.

B: Do they speak Laos, or?

J: Chinese no matter where they go in the world they always set up their own schools for teaching their children how to speak Chinese. Read, write and speak Chinese. Again it's the notion of education. And ah, maintaining the cohesiveness of that culture, their identity. And um, they can always go back to their own. You know, communications, and get the help that they need. But they'll always go out into the community and be part of the community too.

B: Is there a tendency for the Asian community to want to stay together because of where they live? Families near families? Or are they starting to spread out into the city?

J: I think they're a number of them starting to spread out. They're buying their homes outside of the cities. Some of them are buying them in the city.

B: But not necessarily.

J: Again that's controlled.

B: They tend to keep together and (--)

J: If you buy a home and you're going to have your whole extended family live with you. That's the most important thing. The entire group family unit. Grandmother, maybe great-grandmother, grandmother, mother, father, children.

B: In-laws.

J: In-laws, what have you. Cousins, relatives. It's not uncommon ah, have 15-20 people in the immediate family. You know, couple of generations and children of a couple of generations.

B: Is that the traditional pattern of (--)

J: Even in their country.

B: Yeah, but [few words unclear] extended families?

J: Yup.

B: So you live with their mother, or the father's family. I mean the husband or wive's?

J: The wife usually would go live with the husband.

B: Husband's family.

J: Right. Unless of course ah, it would be a very severe hardship on the wives family. In that case the husband would go live there and (B: help) and help out. You know maybe the wife didn't have a father, and by taking the daughter away would really hurt the family. So the husband would go over there and show respect and stay there.

B: The oldest male of the family is usually the head of the family, is that right?

J: Yeah. it's um, this business of equality that we experience in the United States, there was a great article in the Lowell Sun the other day, this Sunday I think it was. There's too much equality in Russia. Did you read that?

B: [Chuckles] No.

J: You didn't. Oh!

B: I was back in Providence for the weekend so I didn't see the Lowell(--)

J: The Lowell Sun had a great article on Russia. And the women were complaining that what's happening is, because there's equality between the races in Russia the natural inclination for the woman that are, you know they're busting their humps out there working side by side with the men, and they're saying, jeese, our real dream in this lifetime is to be able to stay home and raise our children. Okay. And here you have the American women, they're complaining, well our real dream is to get out there and have a career, and have the husband take care of the children.

B: Yeah, but in both societies I think the same thing has happened. That if a woman does have a career she's still respon, she's still the one, in the Soviet Union as well as America, that's got to come home (--)

J: Clean the house and cook dinner.

B: Clean the house, make the dinner [laugh] (J: Sure) look after the kids.

J: Well that's only, you know, that's, that's the way it should be. [laughter]

B: But they're not liberated. I mean a woman thinks she's liberated if she's, you know, free to have a career here and a family too, but my wife doesn't feel that liberated. Let me tell you, she works full time, and she's got three kids. And she's, I have to admit she's the main ah, provider in terms of taking care of them you know, and their needs. Cleaning and cooking.

J: Having, having married a Laotian woman who ah, is very dependent upon, on me for interfacing her needs to the society that she's living in you know, the burden of taking the children to school, picking them up, ah, being in touch with the teacher all falls on my shoulders. It's not something that I wanted, and I don't think it's something that she wanted, but that's the way it is because she doesn't speak English that well. But in terms of ah, taking care of the home and cooking the meals, she wouldn't dream of letting me pick up anything off the floor. You know, hey, get out of here that's my job, you know. And ah, I think that's one reason I married an Asian woman, because I tend to have some male chauvinistic tendencies anyway. And the greatest thing that ever happened to me was marrying an Asian woman. That I'm convinced of, you know. And ah, it's she's by my side every minute of the day. I, as I said right up front, I was married to an American woman, I was an engineer, successful career moving along, stock options with a good company, which I cashed in and ah, used that money to start up my own company. Okay, but with my other, with my first wife there was no way in a hundred years that I would have ever had my own business, because she was not willing to put that kind of an effort into making a business successful. And ah, no one ever dreamed that you'd have to put a hundred and fifty hours a week in in order to make a business successful, but ah, my week I do a hundred five, a hundred and seven hours a week on many many occasions. That's almost like having three jobs, you know, but you have to do that if you want to have a successful business. And um, I've been in touch with my previous wife. She's got her own business now and now she understands ah, you know what it really means to have to get out there and really hustle. But ah, we've had these discussions over the years you know, and ah, her attitude in those days when I was a lot younger was no, no, no, no! You know, I'm not going to sacrifice all the nice things to, to have you have your own business. You can make just as much money by working for someone else as an engineer. You know, if you get in patents, and you know, you're, you're, if you're a good engineer that is, you know. I just never felt complete working for another company. Working for myself I'm not even doing engineering except on the side, you know. And um, I'm having a ball. I do whatever I want, and it's fun.

B: As long as you're working. [laughter]

J: Oh, yeah, it's just our, it's my nature to work. And ah, although in the last three months I haven't done very much. But. We just got back from St. Martins. We went down on vacation.

B: Oh, I was going to ask you, if you go on vacation, what do you do? Can you entrust the ah, store and the restaurant to (--)

J: Yeah, well we have ah (--)

B: Or do you just close up for (--)

J: I have my sister-in-law here. So she takes care of the main store.

B: That's your wife's sister?

J: Yeah. And in the restaurant we have some very good help. Um, we can trust it to them. There's no problem. We had only one vacation in seven years, so. [laughter]

B: That's the problem when you work for yourself.

J: That's the problem. That is the problem. And you tend to be afraid to let the reigns loose you know, to be gone. But this year we took a week up in the mountains in August. We went a week down in St. Martins just last week. And then we took a three day weekend up to Niagara Falls. This is the most vacationing we've done in seven years.

B: How long have you been married?

J: Seven years. (B: Seven years) Seven years, we started the business seven years ago.

B: You had just gotten married.

J: Right.

B: You've got uh, in your store you've got a stock of almost everything you probably need in the restaurant, except maybe fresh, do you have fresh produce in the store?

J: Sure.

B: I'm awful at remembering.

J: You didn't go out into the front part of the store. There's lots of fresh vegetables.

B: About where I come in and turn left.

J: Umhm.

B: Go down there? (J: Yeah) Okay.

J: Lots of fresh vegetables. We do our own butchering on pork. We buy the pork from the U.S.D.A. approved farm. They do the slaughtering, [viscerate?] them. Bring them up to us, and we do all the butchering.

B: Because it's a whole different way of cutting them?

J: Right, right. The pork, we go through five pigs a week.

B: Do you have a an Asian butcher?

J: I had an Asian butcher when we first opened. When we first started doing the pork. And um, I just watched him, two or three pigs later I knew how to do it. And um, it's five years later and I've not done any butchering, because I just keep passing it on to the people that come to work for me. If they work for three or four months, I teach them and they do it. Okay. And the most important important part of the pig anyway is the three layer, the, the bacon. That's the most important part to the Asians. They want the skin, a little bit of layer of fat, some meat, a little other layer of fat, and then more meat. They call it three layer. The three layer meat. That's the most important part of the pig to them. The Cambodians buy the pigs heads, ah, primarily for their ceremonies and ah, their wedding ceremonies. Um, we can buy a pig and there's not one ounce discarded. Every single piece of the pig is sold.

B: Like, I interviewed a, this is back in Rhode Island, a Portuguese farmer. He said the only thing we wasted was the squeal.

J: Yeah, [laugh] that's

B: He said, we even make footballs out of the bladders.

J: Yeah, they use the ah, the bladders they use for ah, they boil it. Get them tender. The wombs, the same thing. The stomachs, the same thing. And they use it in their cooking.

B: So when someone comes into the store to buy a pig, or something, what do they buy? Will they buy an entire (--)

J: Oh, they buy it by the pound. You know whatever we cut up.

B: The white parts by the pound? [Unclear]

J: Yeah, we give them (--) See we're not, by law we're not allowed to sell the innards. We can't even get the innards.

B: Oh!

J: Because it's U.S.D.A. The only thing we can get is liver. Liver and kidneys. Um, we can get hearts.

B: You can get organs, or brains?

J: Ah, not fresh. It has to be processed and ah, the process is they have to boil it first.

B: Oh, okay. I've seen it, but I just didn't know it was boiled.

J: It's boiled first.

B: So what do they do if they want the other stuff?

J: They have to go slaughter it themselves on the farms. And I tell them it's very dangerous, because the only way they're going to insure against the possibility of any of the infectious diseases, you know, the trichinosis and all that, (B: yeah) is to get it from the U.S.D.A. slaughter house.

B: But they won't give you (--)

J: They won't give you the insides. So they go out to the farms, and they slaughter their own pigs.

B: Now did they have that problem in Asia though? With those diseases?

J: Oh, yeah! Sure they always had that problem.

B: Oh, okay. So it's

J: But they, so they're, so they know that when you cook pig you have to cook it well.

B: Probably an acceptable risk for them.

J: Sure, you just cook it well. But see the American in the United States they won't let you even sell it, because they're afraid that the people who buy it from you won't know how to cook it properly. So um, they, they don't rely upon the consumer, they rely upon the entire chain.

B: Right, well that's (--)

J: And they stop it right at the root, which is smart.

B: In. in terms of American culture it is because most of us are so far removed from the food process. We go to the store and it's in a package and we buy it.

J: You come into my store and you see the pig heads sitting in the cooler, if I've got any. Um, people come into my place and they don't know what it is. You know Americans come in and they don't know what the heck is in there. They've never seen a pig in their life.

B: So do you get many Americans come in here?

J: Few, not too many.

B: Just to look around.

J: Just to look around, yeah.

B: Interesting.

J: There are some Americans that are more daring, you know. [laugh] It's fun. I was involved in a, in a project in Bridgeport when we first got married, my wife and I first got married. And ah, the project was, we probably built the first um, temple here on the East coast, in Bridgeport, Conn. Um, the refugees that is. There was a Thai Temple, there were two Thai Temples on the East Coast. One in Washington D.C. and one in New York City. But I know for a fact that we built the first temple for the refugees in Bridgeport. And again I'm somewhat of an oddity. They came to me cause I could speak the language. They asked me to help them. We went to my attorney, and we created a church. Um, went out and bought land. Got donation from everybody in the community, and I got a real education into seeing how they worked between themselves you know. Great deal of distrust from the northern people to the southern people. And all the in fighting, you wouldn't believe it, but it finally got done. We did get the temple up. And ah, it took us about two years before we were able to move the Monk into the temple. He lived with me for, for about four months.

B: Where did they find the Monk? Was he already in the community, or did they have (--)

J: Um, we imported him. Actually we imported him through Canada. And he came in through Canada and we, we, he stayed with me for four months. And he had his ah, his other fam, the rest of his family was out in Utah. That's where they, those people out there brought them in and dropped them off in Utah. And when we wanted them over here, he went out to Utah, picked them up and he became the lead Monk for the, for the temple. The Cambodian's on the other hand, now that's the Laotian Community, there was a lot of in fighting and it was (--)

B: That's in Bridgeport.

J: Yeah, but even in this community, Laotians came to me and asked me to help them. And I'd been through ah, one situation and I said ah, I don't want to go through it again. Um, there is just so much distrust amongst the Laotians from North to South that ah, it was just a troublesome thing to help them. Um, they still don't have their own temple. That's (--)

B: They don't here?

J: No. Not the Laotians. The Cambodians on the other hand, there are only two factions there that um, and there's such a large community of them that one faction alone could handle it. So they do have their own temple over here.

B: Yeah, (--)

J: It was just put up last year.

B: Yeah, I was out there before I came over here.

J: Yeah, in Chelmsford.

B: I think it's in Chelmsford right. It used to be a Knights of Columbus Hall.

J: Yeah, beautiful place.

B: Big.

J: And they, they put it together in ah, in ah, pretty quick order. I guess ah, three years.

B: Yeah.

J: Took them to (--)

B: That's right because I think in 1983 they started at the International Institute.

J: Yeah.

B: They had a hall there. (J: Yup) They had the hall.

J: Well we used to bring the Monk up and bring him to the International. And we used to use the International to do the services for the ah, Laotians.

B: Laotians. Are they going to start a temple?

J: I don't know. I don't know if the Laotians can ever pull it together. Really. The Cambodians ah, had two Monks, and they had them living in back on um, I forget the name of um, the street over there. Something Court. Right in back of Fletcher Street. And they had him living on the third floor. And they were there for almost a year and a half. Their presence in the community ah, held the interest in wanting to put a temple together. And ah, gave it the necessary um, stability and impetus so people would donate on a regular basis. So they were able to buy the building.

B: Yeah, they must have had to raise quite a bit of money

J: Yeah, I don't remember the numbers, but ah, that was the biggest problem with the Laotians. If the Monk wasn't there, out of sight out of mind. You know, and um, as I said I had the Monk living with me for four months. He went into retreat in my own home in Stoneham. And ah, it was really a little bit far away from Lowell. If he were in Lowell, if he were in Lowell it might have worked out differently. But there was, no one would put him up. They didn't, they couldn't even agree on how to collect enough money to pay his rent by keeping him in a single room, whereas the Cambodians could agree.

B: Right. So what fills, is there a gap in religion or (--)

J: Well, the Laotians go out to the Cambodian Temple. (B: unclear) It's the same Buddhism. (B: Umhm) And as long as there is a Monk out at the Cambodian Temple who can speak Thai, they're okay. (B: Oh) Because the Laotians all understand Thai.

B: I know there are what, three, three Monks, plus an American Monk.

J: Yup. Umhm.

B: So one of them speaks(--)

J: I'm pretty sure the old, the old timer, the older Monk (B: Sao Khon) yeah, I believe he speaks Thai. And there's another one that speaks Thai, a younger one. I've never met the American. But I understand that he speaks Cambodian I think.

B: Some, yeah.

J: We had the same situation. When the Monk stayed with me I used to scold them all the time for not following the tenants Of Buddhism.

B: There's only what, a couple of hundred. [laughter]

J: Well, one of the most important things in Buddhism is to eliminate desire.

B: Yes, you're suppose to be celibate.

J: Yeah, well not that kind of desire necessarily, but any desire. Okay. Desire brings heartaches and hardship. And ah,

B: [Unclear] can be damaging.

J: Yeah, so when the Monk was over there, "we got to build a temple." I'd say, "look, you know, that's a big desire that you have." You know [laugh], and that you've got to get rid of that. Another thing is one of the things is they should not sleep more than four inches off the floor. Okay. Um, and when they opened up the temple in Bridgeport, what they did, they went out and bought him a nice fancy bed. And they put a nice mattress on it. And I said, "look Situ that mattress is like six inches number one, and not only that, but the bed is already a foot above the floor." And he says, "no, no it doesn't count there." He said, [laughter] "it's got be from the top of the bed where the mattress sits." I said, "no, come on."

B: Well, they're also (--)

J: You're not suppose to be looking for (--)

B: It's cold here though.

J: Yeah, but that's the whole point.

B: Because they're not suppose to wear underwear under their robes and stuff, but (J: Right) I was talking to the American Monk today and he says they were, he said they were really chastising him for wearing long johns and stuff. He said you wear, you wear a sheet and go outside downtown in January in a sheet. That's what he told them. [Laughs] Because they don't go out too much.

J: Well, they do the right thing, see. [Laughs] They stay there and contemplate, you know.

B: That's right. Well he said he was dealing with a lot of intermediary, you know. Giving kids in school and you know, giving driving lessons, teaching you know, people about what to do if you're stopped by a policeman. Take your registration out. He said he had to go out a lot. I think he was getting cold. [laugh]

J: In those important places. [laugh]

B: Yeah. I thought that was an interesting (--)

J: What else we got over here? I had recently been to ah (--) Oh, they believe, they believe um, in spirits, in ghosts. (B: Right) The old animist beliefs, okay. And recently I went to ah, we had a little bit of a situation in my family. My wife says, "we've got to go see the, the um, Mordo." Mordo means doctor who can see. (B: Oh) Okay. And we've go to go see him, get rid of this bad spirit that's in you. (B: Umhm) Okay. So he put this string and wrapped it on my arm. And he, ah, candles, measured certain parts of my body, and candles and the whole thing. And the string was running into sort of a mock fortress made from um, bamboo sticks. Okay. And the object was to get this bad element out of me, (B: right) down the string and into the fortress. And when it was in the fortress they wrapped it up real quickly and put it into a plastic bag, and would take it out to the river and throw it into the river. You know. And I remember when the Monk came and lived with me in Stoneham. He said to me, "there's something wrong in this house." "So what's wrong?" He said, "there's just something wrong in here." And the Monk that stayed with me, he had ah, the people in the community he came from really believed that he could see beyond. You know, that he could, he could see what was going to happen in the future. Of course he could see what happened in the past. So he closed his eyes. "Oh, there's something very bad in here." He said, "Oh, that's what it is. Get rid of those [diphinbachia?] plants that you have over, that the soil that they're in, someone died in that soil." In order to make him peaceful we had to throw that away. So there, they do come in with a lot of ah, superstitions. We have a group of Jehovah Witnesses now going out witnessing to all the Asians. And ah, I guess that the Jehovah's believe that they're really making converts. But the first minute that anything happens they go running right to the Monk. Okay. Ah, the Asian, or the Buddhist believe, respect all religions. So if you come and tell them that you're a Jehovah Witness, etc., sure they'll respect what you're saying. But when the really push comes to shove, they're right back to Buddha. You know.

B: Do they come into the store looking for certain herbs and things that they use for healing? Do you have these things?

J: They come in, they come into the store looking for the religious articles. The um, incense and the candles. And ah, we keep those things all the time. There, we don't keep many herbs, or anything like that, just tea. They can buy that down in Boston Chinatown. There are a couple of herbalists ah, Vitwa is one and I think ah, Asia, Asia Market is another. They keep all the different herbs.

B: Ah, for what's so called Chinese medicine that's practiced by I guess, all groups.

J: By all of them, yup. Not too long ago there was one girl suffering from cancer. And the father just refused to bring her to American doctors. And she got all her treatment out of Boston. She died, but she probably would have died anyway.

B: She might have, but from what I've heard from just talking to people in community, an Asian Community, they'll try both.

J: Yeah, you know, most of them do.

B: Western and, in terms of medicine, whatever (--)

J: Most of them do. One thing that we're seeing that the children that are being born now are growing very very

TAPE COMES TO END